Effective Ways to Earn Money Online: Maximising Your Earning Potential

Introduction

In today's digital age, more and more people are looking for ways to earn money online. Whether you're a stay-at-home parent, a student, or simply looking for a way to supplement your income, there are many opportunities available to you. However, with so many options out there, it can be overwhelming to know where to start.

That's where this book comes in. "Effective Ways to Earn Money Online: Maximising Your Earning Potential" is a comprehensive guide that will help you navigate the world of online earning. In this book, we'll explore some of the most popular and effective ways to make money online, including freelancing, online surveys, affiliate marketing, and more.

One of the benefits of earning money online is the flexibility it offers. Unlike traditional jobs, online earning allows you to work from anywhere, at any time. Whether you prefer to work early in the morning, late at night, or on weekends, there's an online opportunity that can fit your schedule.

Another benefit of earning money online is the ability to earn passive income. This means that you can earn money even when you're not actively working. For example, if you create an online course or write a book, you can continue to earn money from sales long after you've completed the work.

Of course, earning money online is not without its challenges. One of the biggest challenges is finding legitimate opportunities. Unfortunately, there are many scams and fraudulent schemes out there, so it's important to do your research and be cautious when looking for online earning opportunities.

That's why this book is so valuable. We'll provide you with a comprehensive overview of the most popular and effective ways to make money online, as well as tips for avoiding scams and maximising your earning potential. Whether you're new to the world of online earning or you're looking to expand your existing income streams, this book has something for you.

In the following chapters, we'll explore different strategies for earning money online, including freelancing, online surveys, affiliate marketing, and more. We'll provide you with step-by-step guides for getting started, as well as tips for optimising your earning potential.

We'll also cover some of the common pitfalls and challenges associated with earning money online, such as managing your time effectively, staying motivated, and avoiding burnout. By the end of this book, you'll have a solid understanding of the different ways you can earn money online, as well as the tools and strategies you need to succeed.

Index

1. **Stock trading** - Although stock trading carries risk, it can also be a lucrative way to earn money online. Platforms like Robinhood and E*TRADE offers easy-to-use interfaces for buying and selling stocks.
2. **Social media management** - As social media has become increasingly important for businesses, there's a growing demand for social media managers. If you're savvy with platforms like Facebook, Twitter, and Instagram, you can earn money by managing social media accounts for clients.
3. **Podcast production** - If you have experience in audio editing and production, you can earn money by producing and editing podcasts for clients. Platforms like Popcorn and Anchor offer opportunities to connect with potential clients.
4. **Website design** - If you have a talent for web design, you can earn money by designing websites for clients. Platforms like Upwork and Fiverr offer opportunities to find web design gigs.
5. **App development** - As mobile apps have become increasingly important, there's a growing demand for app developers. If you have experience in coding and app development, you can earn money by creating apps for clients.
6. **Translation** - If you're fluent in a second language, you can earn money by offering translation services. Platforms like Translatorsbase and Gengo offer opportunities to connect with clients who need translation services.

7. **Graphic design** - If you have a talent for graphic design, you can earn money by creating designs for clients. Platforms like 99designs and DesignCrowd offer opportunities to find graphic design gigs.

8. **Online bookkeeping** - Many businesses need help with bookkeeping and accounting tasks, and online bookkeeping services offer a convenient solution. As an online bookkeeper, you can earn money by offering your services remotely.

9. **Online marketplaces** - Platforms like Etsy, eBay, and Amazon also offer opportunities to earn money by selling products online. Whether you're selling handmade crafts, vintage items, or new products, online marketplaces can provide a wide audience and a convenient way to sell your products.

Chapter-1

Stock trading - Although stock trading carries risk, it can also be a lucrative way to earn money online. Platforms like Robinhood and E*TRADE offer easy-to-use interfaces for buying and selling stocks.

Stock trading has become increasingly popular in recent years, with the rise of online trading platforms such as Robinhood and E*TRADE making it easier than ever for individuals to participate in the stock market. While stock trading carries a level of risk, it can also be a lucrative way to earn money online.

Before diving into the world of stock trading, it's important to understand some basic concepts. A stock represents ownership in a company, and when you buy a share of stock, you become a part owner of that company. Stocks are traded on stock exchanges, such as the New York Stock Exchange (NYSE) and NASDAQ.

The price of a stock can fluctuate based on a variety of factors, including company earnings reports, news about the industry or the economy as a whole, and investor sentiment. When the price of a stock goes up, you can sell your shares for a profit. Conversely, if the price of a stock goes down, you may lose money if you sell your shares.

One of the most popular platforms for online stock trading is Robinhood. Robinhood offers a mobile app that allows users to buy and sell stocks, ETFs, and cryptocurrencies without paying any commission fees. This makes it a popular choice for beginners who want to dip their toes into the world of stock trading without incurring high fees.

Another popular platform for online stock trading is ETRADE. ETRADE offers a more robust platform than Robinhood, with more tools and resources for experienced traders. However, this also means that E*TRADE charges commission fees for trades, which can add up over time.

When it comes to stock trading, there are two primary methods: fundamental analysis and technical analysis. Fundamental analysis involves analysing a company's financial statements and other qualitative factors, such as the strength of its management team and its competitive position within the industry. Technical analysis, on the other hand, involves analysing price charts and other quantitative factors to identify patterns and trends in the stock's price movement.

Both fundamental and technical analysis can be useful tools for stock traders. However, it's important to keep in mind that no analysis can predict the future with 100% accuracy. Stock trading always involves a level of risk, and it's important to have a solid understanding of the risks before investing your money.

One way to mitigate risk when stock trading is to diversify your portfolio. This means investing in a variety of different stocks across different industries, rather than putting all of your money into one stock. Diversification can help spread out risk and minimise the impact of any one stock's price movement on your overall portfolio.

Another important factor to consider when stock trading is your time horizon. If you're a short-term trader, you may be more focused on identifying short-term trends and making quick profits. If you're a long-term investor, on the other hand, you may be more interested in identifying high-quality companies that you believe will grow over time.

Finally, it's important to have a solid understanding of the tax implications of stock trading. When you sell a stock for a profit, you'll typically owe capital gains tax on that profit. The amount of tax you'll owe depends on how long you held the stock before selling it, as well as your tax bracket.

In conclusion, stock trading can be a lucrative way to earn money online, but it's important to understand the risks involved before investing your money. Platforms like Robinhood and E*TRADE offers easy-to-use interfaces for buying and selling stocks, and both fundamental and technical analysis can be useful tools for stock traders. It's also important to diversify your portfolio, consider your time horizon, and understand the tax implications of stock trading. With the right approach and a solid understanding of the risks involved, stock trading can be a rewarding way to build wealth over time. However, it's important to always do your own research and make informed decisions when it comes to buying and selling stocks.

It's also worth noting that stock trading is not a get-rich-quick scheme. It requires patience, discipline, and a long-term mindset. While it's possible to make quick profits in the stock market, it's also possible to lose money if you're not careful. It's important to set realistic expectations and to always have a plan in place before making any trades.

Another important factor to consider when stock trading is market volatility. The stock market can be unpredictable, and prices can fluctuate rapidly based on a variety of factors. This can create both opportunities and risks for investors. It's important to stay up-to-date on market news and to be prepared to adjust your strategy as needed in response to changing market conditions.

Overall, stock trading can be a rewarding way to earn money online, but it's important to approach it with caution and to always do your own research before investing your money. With the right mindset, strategy, and tools, stock trading can be a powerful way to build wealth over time.

Chapter-2

<u>Social media management</u> - As social media has become increasingly important for businesses, there's a growing demand for social media managers. If you're savvy with platforms like Facebook, Twitter, and Instagram, you can earn money by managing social media accounts for clients.

Social media has become an integral part of modern business, with many companies using social media platforms like Facebook, Twitter, and Instagram to connect with customers, promote their products and services, and build their brand. As a result, there's a growing demand for social media managers who can help businesses navigate the complex world of social media marketing.

If you're savvy with social media platforms and have a knack for marketing and communication, you can earn money by managing social media accounts for clients. Social media managers are responsible for creating and executing social media strategies, creating content, engaging with followers, and analysing performance metrics to ensure that social media campaigns are effective.

One of the key skills required for social media management is the ability to create engaging content that resonates with your target audience. This includes developing a content calendar, brainstorming ideas for posts, and creating visual assets like images and videos. It's also important to have excellent communication skills, as social media managers are often responsible for responding to customer inquiries and engaging with followers in a timely and professional manner.

In addition to creating content, social media managers are responsible for monitoring social media platforms for mentions of their clients' brand, responding to customer inquiries and complaints, and engaging with followers to build relationships and promote the brand. They may also be responsible for running paid social media campaigns, analysing performance metrics, and adjusting their strategies as needed to improve results.

There are a variety of tools and resources available to help social media managers streamline their workflow and improve their results. Many social media platforms offer built-in analytics tools that allow you to track engagement, reach, and other performance metrics. There are also a number of third-party tools available, such as Hootsuite and Buffer, that allow you to manage multiple social media accounts from a single dashboard and schedule posts in advance.

When it comes to pricing social media management services, there are a few different models to consider. Some social media managers charge a flat monthly fee for their services, while others charge hourly rates. It's important to establish clear expectations with clients upfront, including how often you'll post, what types of content you'll create, and how you'll measure results.

One of the key benefits of social media management is the flexibility it offers. As a social media manager, you can work from anywhere with an internet connection, making it a great option for freelancers and digital nomads. However, it's important to stay organised and disciplined when working remotely, as social media management can be a time-consuming and demanding job.

To be successful as a social media manager, it's important to stay up-to-date on the latest social media trends and best practices. This may include attending conferences and networking events, participating in online communities, and following thought leaders in the industry. It's also important to be adaptable and willing to experiment with new strategies and tactics in order to achieve the best possible results.

Overall, social media management can be a rewarding and lucrative way to earn money online. If you have a talent for creating engaging content, building relationships with followers, and analysing performance metrics, you may be well-suited for a career in social media management. With the right skills, tools, and mindset, you can help businesses succeed in the fast-paced and ever-changing world of social media marketing.

Chapter-3

Podcast production - If you have experience in audio editing and production, you can earn money by producing and editing podcasts for clients. Platforms like Popcorn and Anchor offer opportunities to connect with potential clients.

Podcasts have exploded in popularity in recent years, with millions of people tuning in to their favourite shows each week. As a result, there's a growing demand for podcast producers who can help businesses and individuals create high-quality audio content that resonates with listeners.

If you have experience in audio editing and production, you can earn money by producing and editing podcasts for clients. This can include everything from recording and editing audio, to writing and producing content, to managing distribution and promotion.

One of the key skills required for podcast production is audio editing. This involves using software like Audacity or Adobe Audition to edit audio recordings, removing background noise, adjusting volume levels, and adding sound effects and music. It's also important to have a good ear for audio quality, as well as the ability to mix and master audio tracks to ensure a professional sound.

In addition to audio editing, podcast producers are often responsible for creating content for their clients' shows. This can include researching and developing topics, writing scripts, and booking guests. It's important to have excellent communication and organisational skills, as podcast production often involves coordinating schedules and deadlines with multiple parties.

Once the audio content is recorded and edited, podcast producers are responsible for managing distribution and promotion. This can involve uploading episodes to podcast hosting platforms like Anchor or Buzzsprout, as well as promoting episodes on social media and other digital channels to attract listeners.

There are a variety of tools and resources available to help podcast producers streamline their workflow and improve their results. In addition to audio editing software, there are also tools available to help with content development and distribution, such as Trello and Canva. Many podcast hosting platforms also offer built-in analytics tools that allow you to track audience engagement and other performance metrics.

When it comes to pricing podcast production services, there are a few different models to consider. Some podcast producers charge a flat fee per episode, while others charge hourly rates. It's important to establish clear expectations with clients upfront, including how many episodes you'll produce, what types of content you'll create, and how you'll measure results.

Platforms like Popcorn and Anchor offer opportunities to connect with potential clients and promote your podcast production services. It's important to create a strong online presence and to showcase your skills and expertise in order to attract clients and build your reputation as a top-notch podcast producer.

One of the key benefits of podcast production is the flexibility it offers. As a podcast producer, you can work from anywhere with an internet connection, making it a great option for freelancers and digital nomads. However, it's important to stay organised and disciplined when working remotely, as podcast production can be a time-consuming and demanding job.

To be successful as a podcast producer, it's important to stay up-to-date on the latest podcasting trends and best practices. This may include attending conferences and networking events, participating in online communities, and following thought leaders in the industry. It's also important to be adaptable and willing to experiment with new strategies and tactics in order to achieve the best possible results.

Overall, podcast production can be a rewarding and lucrative way to earn money online. If you have a talent for audio editing, content creation, and promotion, you may be well-suited for a career in podcast production. With the right skills, tools, and mindset, you can help businesses and individuals succeed in the exciting and rapidly-growing world of podcasting.

Chapter-4

Website design - If you have a talent for web design, you can earn money by designing websites for clients. Platforms like Upwork and Fiverr offer opportunities to find web design gigs.

In today's digital age, having a professional website is crucial for businesses of all sizes. As a result, there is a growing demand for talented web designers who can create stunning and functional websites that meet the needs of their clients. If you have a talent for web design, you can earn money by designing websites for clients.

To succeed as a web designer, it's important to have a strong understanding of design principles, as well as experience with web design tools and software. This includes knowledge of HTML, CSS, and JavaScript, as well as popular design tools like Adobe Photoshop and Sketch. It's also important to stay up-to-date on the latest design trends and best practices in order to create websites that are visually appealing, user-friendly, and optimised for search engines.

There are many platforms available that can help you find web design gigs and connect with potential clients. Upwork and Fiverr are two popular platforms that allow freelancers to create profiles, showcase their skills and experience, and bid on job postings. These platforms also offer built-in messaging and payment systems to facilitate communication and payment between clients and designers.

When it comes to pricing web design services, there are several different models to consider. Some designers charge a flat fee for each project, while others charge hourly rates. It's important to establish clear expectations with clients upfront, including the scope of the project, the number of revisions included in the price, and the timeline for completion.

In addition to designing websites from scratch, web designers may also be responsible for maintaining and updating existing websites. This can involve making minor design tweaks, updating content, and ensuring that the website is running smoothly and is secure. It's important to have a good understanding of website maintenance and security best practices in order to provide high-quality services to clients.

In order to succeed as a web designer, it's also important to have strong communication and project management skills. This includes the ability to communicate effectively with clients, manage timelines and deadlines, and coordinate with other members of the project team. It's also important to be adaptable and flexible, as client needs and project requirements may change over time.

There are a variety of resources available to help web designers improve their skills and stay up-to-date on the latest design trends and best practices. This may include taking online courses and tutorials, attending conferences and networking events, and following thought leaders in the industry. It's also important to build a portfolio of your work in order to showcase your skills and attract potential clients.

One of the key benefits of web design is the flexibility it offers. As a web designer, you can work from anywhere with an internet connection, making it a great option for freelancers and digital nomads. However, it's important to stay organised and disciplined when working remotely, as web design can be a time-consuming and demanding job.

In conclusion, web design is a lucrative and rewarding way to earn money online. If you have a talent for design and a passion for creating beautiful and functional websites, you may be well-suited for a career in web design. With the right skills, tools, and mindset, you can help businesses and individuals succeed in the competitive world of online marketing. Platforms like Upwork and Fiverr offer great opportunities to find web design gigs and build your reputation as a top-notch web designer.

Chapter-5

<u>App development</u> - As mobile apps have become increasingly important, there's a growing demand for app developers. If you have experience in coding and app development, you can earn money by creating apps for clients.

Mobile apps have revolutionised the way we interact with our smartphones and devices, and their importance has only increased with time. As a result, there has been a significant rise in the demand for app developers who can create innovative and engaging mobile applications for a variety of platforms.

App development is a complex and diverse field that requires a range of skills, including coding, design, testing, and project management. App developers need to have a deep understanding of programming languages such as Java, Kotlin, Swift, and C#, as well as knowledge of app architecture, user interface design, and database management.

For those with experience in coding and app development, creating mobile apps for clients can be a lucrative way to earn money. The process typically involves working with a client to understand their specific requirements and developing a customised app that meets their needs.

Before starting a project, app developers need to have a clear understanding of the client's objectives and target audience. This includes gathering information about the client's business or organisation, their competitors, and the market trends in their industry.

Once the app developer has a clear idea of the client's needs, they can begin the development process. This involves creating wireframes, designing the user interface, and writing the code for the app's functionality.

During the development process, it's important to test the app thoroughly to ensure that it functions as intended and meets the client's requirements. This includes testing the app on multiple devices and platforms, as well as conducting usability testing to ensure that the app is intuitive and easy to use.

Once the app is complete, it's important to ensure that it's properly optimised for the app stores. This involves creating a compelling app description, selecting the right keywords, and optimising the app's images and videos.

Once the app is live in the app stores, the app developer can earn money through a variety of monetization strategies. This includes selling the app directly to users, offering in-app purchases, or using ads to generate revenue.

Another option for app developers is to create apps as a service. This involves creating a platform or service that allows users to create and manage their own mobile apps. App developers can earn money by charging a subscription fee for access to the platform, as well as offering additional services such as app store optimization, marketing, and analytics.

App developers can also earn money by creating apps for other businesses or organisations. This includes creating custom apps for businesses that need a specific solution, such as a sales or inventory management app. App developers can also create white-label apps that can be rebranded and customised for multiple clients.

Overall, app development is a challenging but rewarding field that offers a range of opportunities for those with the right skills and experience. With the increasing demand for mobile apps and the growth of the app economy, there has never been a better time to become an app developer.

To succeed as an app developer, it's important to have a deep understanding of coding languages, app architecture, and user interface design. It's also important to stay up-to-date with the latest trends and technologies in the field, as well as being able to adapt to changing client needs.

In addition to technical skills, app developers also need to have strong communication and project management skills. This includes being able to work closely with clients to understand their needs, as well as managing timelines and budgets to ensure that projects are completed on time and within budget.

In conclusion, app development is a rapidly growing field that offers a range of opportunities for those with the right skills and experience. With the increasing demand for mobile apps, there has never been a better time to become an app developer and earn money by creating innovative and engaging mobile applications for clients.

Chapter-6

Translation - If you're fluent in a second language, you can earn money by offering translation services. Platforms like Translatorsbase and Gengo offer opportunities to connect with clients who need translation services.

In today's globalised world, the ability to communicate in multiple languages is becoming increasingly important. As a result, there is a growing demand for translation services, which presents a great opportunity for those who are fluent in a second language to earn money.

Translation involves the process of converting written or spoken content from one language to another while preserving the meaning and tone of the original message. This can include translating documents, websites, software, marketing materials, legal documents, and more.

Platforms such as Translatorsbase and Gengo provide opportunities for translators to connect with clients who require translation services. These platforms allow translators to create a profile, showcase their skills and experience, and bid on translation projects that match their expertise.

To succeed as a translator, it's important to have a deep understanding of both the source and target languages. This includes having a strong command of grammar, vocabulary, and syntax, as well as an understanding of cultural nuances and context.

In addition to language skills, translators also need to have excellent research skills and attention to detail. This includes being able to conduct research on the subject matter being translated, as well as checking for accuracy and consistency in the translated content.

Another important factor in translation is the use of specialised software and tools. This includes translation memory software, which can help speed up the translation process by storing commonly used phrases and terminology for future use.

When offering translation services, it's important to establish clear communication with the client to ensure that their needs are met. This includes discussing project timelines, requirements, and expectations upfront, as well as providing regular updates on the progress of the project.

In terms of payment, translators can earn money through a variety of methods, including per-word or per-page rates, hourly rates, or project-based rates. Rates can vary depending on the complexity of the content being translated, the languages involved, and the deadlines required.

In addition to working with clients on translation projects, translators can also earn money by creating their own content in multiple languages. This can include writing blog posts, articles, and other content for businesses or individuals who require multilingual content.

Overall, translation offers a great opportunity for those who are fluent in a second language to earn money by providing valuable services to clients who require accurate and high-quality translations. With the growth of the global economy and the increasing importance of communication across languages and cultures, there has never been a better time to offer translation services.

To succeed as a translator, it's important to have a deep understanding of both the source and target languages, as well as a strong attention to detail and the ability to use specialised software and tools. It's also important to establish clear communication with clients upfront and to have a flexible and adaptable approach to different projects and requirements.

Translation is a highly competitive field, and it's important to continuously improve skills and knowledge in order to stay ahead of the competition. This includes staying up-to-date with the latest technologies and trends in the industry, as well as seeking out professional development opportunities such as courses and certifications.

In conclusion, translation is a valuable and in-demand service that offers a great opportunity for those who are fluent in a second language to earn money. With the growth of the global economy and the increasing importance of communication across languages and cultures, the demand for translation services is only expected to continue to grow. Platforms like Translatorsbase and Gengo offer an easy way for translators to connect with clients and find translation projects that match their skills and expertise.

Chapter-7

<u>*Graphic design*</u> - If you have a talent for graphic design, you can earn money by creating designs for clients. Platforms like 99designs and DesignCrowd offer opportunities to find graphic design gigs.

In today's digital age, graphic design plays a vital role in creating visually appealing and engaging content for businesses and individuals alike. If you have a talent for graphic design, there are many opportunities to earn money by creating designs for clients.

Graphic design involves the process of creating visual content using software such as Adobe Photoshop, Illustrator, and InDesign. This can include designing logos, business cards, websites, social media graphics, marketing materials, and more.

Platforms like 99designs and DesignCrowd offer opportunities for graphic designers to find gigs and connect with clients who require graphic design services. These platforms allow designers to create a profile, showcase their work, and bid on design projects that match their expertise.

To succeed as a graphic designer, it's important to have a strong understanding of design principles, such as colour theory, typography, and composition. It's also important to have a strong grasp of design software and tools, as well as the ability to stay up-to-date with the latest design trends and technologies.

In addition to technical skills, graphic designers also need to have excellent communication and collaboration skills. This includes being able to listen to clients' needs, provide feedback and suggestions, and work with clients to ensure that their design needs are met.

When offering graphic design services, it's important to establish clear communication with clients to ensure that their needs and expectations are met. This includes discussing project timelines, requirements, and expectations upfront, as well as providing regular updates on the progress of the project.

In terms of payment, graphic designers can earn money through a variety of methods, including hourly rates, project-based rates, or flat fees. Rates can vary depending on the complexity of the project, the level of experience of the designer, and the deadlines required.

In addition to working with clients on design projects, graphic designers can also earn money by creating and selling their own designs. This can include selling designs on platforms such as Etsy or creating their own online store to sell designs.

Overall, graphic design offers a great opportunity for those with a talent for design to earn money by providing valuable services to clients who require visually appealing and engaging designs. With the growth of digital media and the increasing importance of creating visually appealing content, there has never been a better time to offer graphic design services.

To succeed as a graphic designer, it's important to have a strong understanding of design principles and software tools, as well as excellent communication and collaboration skills. It's also important to stay up-to-date with the latest design trends and technologies and to continuously improve skills and knowledge in order to stay ahead of the competition.

Graphic design is a highly competitive field, and it's important to have a strong portfolio and online presence in order to attract clients. This includes showcasing previous work and testimonials from satisfied clients, as well as having a professional and polished online portfolio and social media presence.

In conclusion, graphic design offers a great opportunity for those with a talent for design to earn money by providing valuable services to clients who require visually appealing and engaging designs. Platforms like 99designs and DesignCrowd offer an easy way for designers to find gigs and connect with clients who require graphic design services. To succeed as a graphic designer, it's important to have a strong understanding of design principles and software tools, as well as excellent communication and collaboration skills. With the growth of digital media and the increasing importance of creating visually appealing content, the demand for graphic design services is only expected to continue to grow.

Chapter-8

Online bookkeeping - Many businesses need help with bookkeeping and accounting tasks, and online bookkeeping services offer a convenient solution. As an online bookkeeper, you can earn money by offering your services remotely.

Bookkeeping and accounting are essential tasks for any business, but not all businesses have the time, resources, or expertise to handle them in-house. This is where online bookkeeping services come in - offering a convenient and affordable solution for businesses of all sizes.

As an online bookkeeper, you can earn money by providing bookkeeping services remotely. This involves keeping track of a business's financial transactions, such as sales, expenses, and payments, and preparing financial reports and statements.

To succeed as an online bookkeeper, it's important to have a strong understanding of accounting principles and software tools, as well as excellent communication and organisational skills. Many businesses use cloud-based accounting software such as QuickBooks or Xero, so proficiency in these tools is often essential.

Online bookkeeping services can include a variety of tasks, such as recording and categorising transactions, reconciling bank accounts, preparing financial statements, and providing reports for tax purposes. As an online bookkeeper, you may also provide advice and guidance on financial matters, such as budgeting and cash flow management.

To get started as an online bookkeeper, it's important to establish a strong online presence and market your services effectively. This can include creating a website or social media profiles, showcasing your qualifications and experience, and offering competitive rates.

Many online bookkeepers offer their services on a freelance or contract basis, allowing them to work with multiple clients and set their own hours. This can provide flexibility and autonomy, as well as the opportunity to work with a variety of businesses in different industries.

When working with clients as an online bookkeeper, it's important to establish clear communication and expectations upfront. This includes discussing project timelines, requirements, and expectations, as well as providing regular updates on the progress of the project.

In terms of payment, online bookkeepers can earn money through a variety of methods, including hourly rates, project-based rates, or flat fees. Rates can vary depending on the complexity of the project, the level of experience of the bookkeeper, and the deadlines required.

Overall, online bookkeeping offers a great opportunity for those with a background in accounting or bookkeeping to earn money by providing valuable services to businesses who require financial management support. With the growth of cloud-based accounting software and the increasing need for businesses to outsource bookkeeping tasks, there has never been a better time to offer online bookkeeping services.

To succeed as an online bookkeeper, it's important to have a strong understanding of accounting principles and software tools, as well as excellent communication and organisational skills. It's also important to stay up-to-date with the latest accounting trends and technologies and to continuously improve skills and knowledge in order to stay ahead of the competition.

Online bookkeeping is a highly competitive field, and it's important to have a strong online presence and reputation in order to attract clients. This includes showcasing previous work and testimonials from satisfied clients, as well as having a professional and polished online portfolio and social media presence.

In conclusion, online bookkeeping offers a great opportunity for those with a background in accounting or bookkeeping to earn money by providing valuable services to businesses who require financial management support. To succeed as an online bookkeeper, it's important to have a strong understanding of accounting principles and software tools, as well as excellent communication and organisational skills. With the growth of cloud-based accounting software and the increasing need for businesses to outsource bookkeeping tasks, the demand for online bookkeeping services is only expected to continue to grow.

Chapter-9

Online marketplaces - Platforms like Etsy, eBay, and Amazon also offer opportunities to earn money by selling products online. Whether you're selling handmade crafts, vintage items, or new products, online marketplaces can provide a wide audience and a convenient way to sell your products.

Online marketplaces such as Etsy, eBay, and Amazon have become increasingly popular for individuals looking to earn money by selling products online. Whether you are selling handmade crafts, vintage items, or new products, online marketplaces offer a convenient way to reach a large audience and generate income.

To get started selling on these platforms, you will typically need to create an account and set up a store or listing. This involves creating a profile, selecting a payment method, and providing product information and images. Some platforms may also require you to meet certain standards or criteria before you can start selling, such as verifying your identity or meeting specific product standards.

Once you have set up your store or listings, you can begin promoting your products and attracting customers. This can involve optimising your product listings for search engines, using social media to promote your products, and offering discounts or promotions to attract customers.

One of the key advantages of selling on online marketplaces is the ability to reach a large and diverse audience. These platforms typically have millions of users worldwide, which can help you to generate sales and grow your business. In addition, online marketplaces often provide tools and resources to help you manage your sales and keep track of your finances, such as sales reports, analytics, and payment processing services.

However, there are also some challenges to selling on online marketplaces, including competition from other sellers and platform fees. Many online marketplaces charge fees for listing products or taking a percentage of each sale, which can reduce your profits. Additionally, with so many sellers competing for customers' attention, it can be difficult to stand out and attract sales.

To succeed on online marketplaces, it's important to differentiate your products and provide excellent customer service. This can involve offering unique or high-quality products, providing detailed product descriptions and images, and responding promptly to customer inquiries and concerns.

Another key factor in succeeding on online marketplaces is pricing your products competitively. This involves researching the market to determine what similar products are selling for and adjusting your prices accordingly. It's also important to factor in any platform fees or shipping costs when setting your prices.

In addition to selling on established online marketplaces, there are also opportunities to create your own online store or sell products through your own website or social media channels. This can provide more control over the branding and customer experience, but also requires more effort and resources to set up and promote.

To create your own online store, you will typically need to choose a platform or website builder, select a payment processor, and design your store and product listings. This can involve learning new skills or working with a designer or developer to create a professional and effective online store.

Once your online store is set up, you can promote your products using social media, email marketing, and other channels. It's also important to provide excellent customer service and maintain high-quality products to generate repeat business and positive reviews.

In conclusion, online marketplaces offer a convenient and accessible way to earn money by selling products online. Whether you are selling handmade crafts, vintage items, or new products, these platforms provide a large and diverse audience and a range of tools and resources to help you manage your sales and grow your business. While there are challenges to selling on online marketplaces, such as competition and fees, there are also many opportunities to differentiate your products and provide excellent customer service to generate sales and build a successful business.